PHONICS

101 Things Every 1ST GRADER Should Know About PHONICS

Contributing Writer

Lisa Trumbauer

Consultant

Dr. Leslie Anne Perry

Lisa Trumbauer is the *New York Times* best-selling author of *A Practical Guide to Dragons.* She has written about 300 books for children, including novels, picture books, and nonfiction books. She's also authored a number of activity books for the early grades. A graduate of the University of Maryland, she received a degree in journalism, with a minor in education. Lisa lives in New Jersey with her husband, Dave, two moody cats, and a dog named Blue.

Dr. Leslie Anne Perry has been teaching public school for 13 years. Currently, she is a professor in the department of curriculum and instruction at East Tennessee State University, where she teaches language arts and children's literature courses. She also serves as the coordinator for the M.Ed. in elementary education program. She is the author of *Primary Reading and Writing Activities for Every Month of the School Year* and has had 65 articles published in 55 different journals and magazines.

Illustrations by **George Ulrich**

Picture credits: **Comstock RF; Corbis RF; Image Club Graphics; PhotoDisc; PIL Collection; StockByte**

Louis Weber, CEO
Publications International, Ltd.
7373 North Cicero Avenue
Lincolnwood, Illinois 60712

www.myactiveminds.com

ISBN-13: 978-1-4127-1617-8
ISBN-10: 1-4127-1617-9

Manufactured in China.

8 7 6 5 4 3 2 1

Contents

Follow the Phonics Path

Dear Parents:

First grade is a time of discovery, and the skills children developed in kindergarten are broadened and expanded. Children will begin to learn to think critically, especially while they read. The reading process will become more active, yet children

still must be able to recognize letters and frequently used words. While this recognition is important, children must also associate specific letters and combinations of letters with their corresponding sounds. By putting these letter sounds together, children will be able to read new words. Recognizing letter sounds and spelling patterns is what phonics is all about!

In this workbook, you will find 101 phonics activities that encourage your child to think about letters and the sounds they make. Each activity focuses on a different letter or spelling pattern and its sound. The fun and interesting nature of each activity will help your child understand these letters and sounds. This workbook begins with simple, easy-to-recognize consonant sounds and graduates to more complex letter patterns. Children will be able to build upon their phonics knowledge and apply what they've already learned to new sounds.

Every activity clearly explains the phonics skill being taught. You will also find skill keys written especially for you, the parent, at the end of each activity. These skill keys quickly explain what your child is learning in each activity. On some pages, you'll also find suggestions for additional hands-on activities that you and your child may do to reinforce skills. As you and your child engage in these activities, your child will see how phonics can be applied outside of this workbook.

As children explore phonics, they must learn to recognize letters and sounds both visually and through listening. It may be beneficial to review sounds by asking your child to close his or her eyes and listen while you say words from an activity aloud. Have your child identify the letters and sounds in the words you say. Next, you can have your child repeat the words with you while pointing to the words on the page. Your child will be making important connections between letters and sounds, which is crucial for phonics learning.

The activities in this book have been designed to build your child's confidence as he or she completes each task independently. It might be necessary, however, for you to read the instructions out loud. Whether an activity calls for matching, writing in a missing letter, solving a puzzle, or completing a maze, it will help your child develop the phonics skills necessary to become a more fluent reader as well as a better speller. Gently prompt your child if he or she needs help, and when an activity is completed, congratulate your child on a job well done. Enjoy your time together as your child enhances his or her first-grade phonics skills.

What Is Phonics?

This song is about phonics. It is sung to the tune of "Mary Had a Little Lamb." Sing it with your family! Sing it with your friends!

Phonics tells us letter sounds,
    Letter sounds,
    Letter sounds!
Phonics tells us letter sounds,
The letter sounds in words.

The alphabet has 26 letters,
    26 letters,
    26 letters!
The alphabet has 26 letters,
Each with its own sound.

21 letters are consonants,
    Consonants,
    Consonants!
21 letters are consonants,
    Like B and D and G.

Five more letters are the vowels,
    Are the vowels,
    Are the vowels!
Five more letters are the vowels,
    A, E, I, O, U.

Put letters together, and what do you get?
    Words like **cat,**
    And **dog** and **pet!**
Put letters together, and what do you get?
    Words that help us read!

Look at the last verse.

Find a word for an animal with a short **a** sound, like **bat.** Write it here.

_____

Find a word for an animal that begins with the **d** sound, like **duck.** Write it here. _____

Which letters make up your first name? Write your name here:

_____

Parents: Sing the song with your child. Guide your child in finding the words **cat** and **dog** in the last verse. Then help your child write his or her first name in the space.

Skill: Recalling the letters of the alphabet and their sounds

Answers on page 121.

Clubhouse Phonics

Look around the clubhouse. Say the word for each picture. What letter does each word start with—**b, c, d,** or **f?** Write the correct letter on the line.

C alendar

d oor

f ish

b oat

d esk

b ox

c up

Parents: Help your child practice recognizing the sounds represented by the consonants **b, c, d,** and **f** by locating items in your home that begin with these sounds.

Skill: Reviewing the words and sounds made by the consonants **b, c, d,** and **f**

Answers on page 121.

Which Letter Is Better?

Say the word for each picture. Circle the letter you hear at the beginning of the word.

h j (k)

(g) h k

g h (k)

j (g) h

(h) g j

k h (j)

Answers on page 121.

Mouse Maze

Help the mouse get through the maze. Say the name of each picture on the maze paths. Find the path with words that begin with **l, m, n,** or **p.** Draw a line along this path until you reach the cheese.

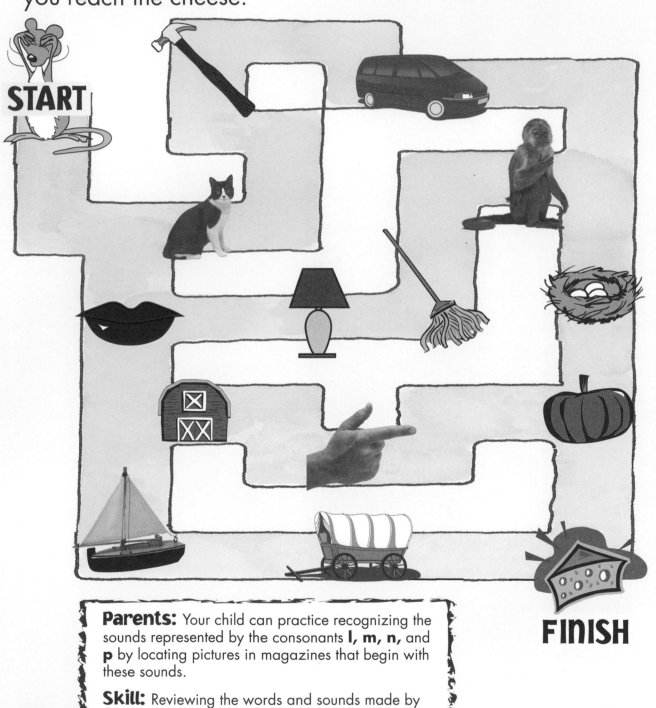

START

FINISH

Parents: Your child can practice recognizing the sounds represented by the consonants **l, m, n,** and **p** by locating pictures in magazines that begin with these sounds.

Skill: Reviewing the words and sounds made by the consonants **l, m, n,** and **p**

Answer on page 121.

The Queen Rules!

The queen only likes things that begin with the letters **q, r, s,** and **t.** Say the word for each picture. Listen to the beginning sound. Draw a line from the picture to the letter it starts with.

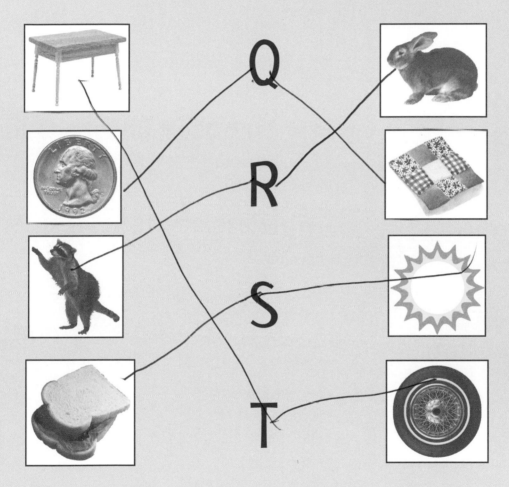

Q

R

S

T

Parents: Your child can practice recognizing the sounds represented by the consonants **q, r, s,** and **t** by locating pictures in magazines that begin with these sounds. Point out to your child that the letter **q** is usually followed by the letter **u.** The letters **qu** together form the sound **kw,** like in **quilt,** or **k,** like in **unique.**

Skill: Reviewing the words and sounds made by the consonants **q, r, s,** and **t**

Answers on page 121.

Watch That Word!

Say the word for each picture. Which letter is missing? Is it the letter **v, w, x, y,** or **z?** (Hint: Sometimes the letter **x** comes at the end of a word and sounds like **ks.**) Write the missing letter for each word on the line.

_W_ agon

_Y_ an

_Y_ arn

_Z_ ipper

Parents: Your child can practice recognizing the sounds represented by the consonants **v, w, x, y,** and **z** by locating pictures in magazines or objects around your home that begin with these sounds.

Skill: Reviewing the words and sounds made by the consonants **v, w, x, y,** and **z**

fo X

V iolin

Y o- Y o

Z ebra

X -ray

W alrus

Answers on page 121.

Handy Dandy Words

When you read, you will come across some words more often than others. It is handy to learn these words. The words in the box are "handy dandy words." Find and circle these words in the poem below.

| a | and | are | in | is | it | of | the | to | you |

Handy Dandy Words

If you want your reading to flow,
Handy words are great to know,
Words like **the** and **of** and **you,**
Are found in books and magazines, too.
And knowing words like **a** and **it**
Is sure to make a really big hit.
Handy words are words you see,
Over and over whenever you read.

Parents: If the Handy Dandy Words are taught along with phonics, your child's reading will be much more fluent. In school, "handy dandy words" are called "high-frequency" or "sight" words. To review the words, you can write each one on an index card. Write a sentence featuring the word on the reverse side of the card. Your child can use the cards to practice reading these important words.

Skill: Reviewing high-frequency words

Answers on page 121.

A Wagon Full of Words

The letter **a** can make the short **a** sound, like in **wagon.** Fill this wagon with short **a** words. Write the letter **a** to complete each word.

f A n

c A p

p A n

A nt

A lligator

A pple

b A t

c A t

Answers on page 121.

Let's Go Sledding!

The letter **e** can make the short **e** sound, like in **sled.** Say the word for each picture. Circle the pictures with the short **e** sound.

Parents: Your child can listen for short vowel sounds when you are reading to him or her. Since many words in the English language contain short vowels, you will find plenty of short vowel sounds in any book or magazine.

Skill: Recognizing the short **e** sound

Answers on page 121.

Hidden Picture fish

The letter **i** can make the short **i** sound, like in **pig.** Read each word in the picture. If you hear the short **i** sound, color the space orange. If you don't hear the short **i** sound, color the space blue.

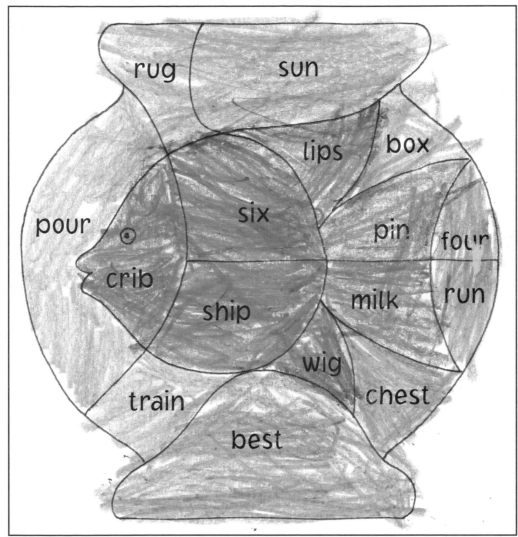

rug

sun

lips

box

pour

six

pin

four

crib

milk

run

ship

wig

chest

train

best

Parents: As you complete the activity with your child, say the word for the hidden picture. Ask your child if the word has the short **i** sound. (**Fish**—yes.) Your child can listen for short vowel sounds when you are reading to him or her. Since many words in the English language contain short vowels, you will find plenty of short vowel sounds in any book or magazine.

Skill: Recognizing the short **i** sound

Answers on page 121.

A Box of O's

The letter **o** can make the short **o** sound, like in **box.** Say the word for each picture. If you hear the short **o** sound, draw a line from the picture to the box. If you don't hear the short **o** sound, draw an **X** through the picture.

18

Answers on page 121.

Jump on the Bus!

The letter **u** can make the short **u** sound, like in **bus.** Only words with the short **u** sound can get the bus to school. Which words are they? Say the words on the path. Draw a line to follow the words with short **u** sounds.

Parents: Because this activity does not have pictures to guide children, read each word with your child. Ask your child the following question for each word: "Does this word have the **u** sound, like in **bus?**" If it does, have your child draw a line from one short **u** word to the next until the school bus has made its way to the school at the bottom of the page.

Skill: Recognizing the short **u** sound

Answer on page 122.

Rain, Rain, Go Away!

The letter **a** can make the long **a** sound, like in **rain.** Say the word in each raindrop. If you hear the long **a** sound, color the raindrop blue. If you don't hear the long **a,** draw an **X** through the raindrop.

rake

lamp

snake

apple

train

door

cake

gate

car

brain

Answers on page 122.

Feel the Beat!

The letter **e** can make the long **e** sound, like in **feel** and **beat.** Say the word for each picture. In each space, write in the missing letter **e.**

___ agle

tr ___ ___

qu ___ ___ n

b ___ agle

f ___ ___ t

j ___ ans

s ___ al

Skill: Recognizing the long **e** sound

Answers on page 122. 21

Oh, No!

The letter **o** can make the long **o** sound, like in **oat.** Say the words for these pictures. Circle the pictures with long **o** sounds.

Answers on page 122.

The I's Have It!

The letter **i** can make the long **i** sound, like in **hive.** Say the name of each picture in the row. If the word has the long **i** sound, circle the picture.

Answers on page 122.

Unicorns Know Best

The letter **u** can make the long **u** sound, like in **unicorn.** Say the words for these pictures. Circle the correct long **u** word for each picture.

cube cub

tub tube

blue bell

glob glue

foot fruit

suit sit

Parents: Explain to your child that the letter **u** can actually stand for two different sounds in words. The sound in the word **cube** is not the same as the sound in the word **fruit.** In the word **cube,** the **u** "says" its name. In the word **fruit,** the long **u** sound is more like **oo** in the word **zoo.**

Skill: Recognizing the long **u** sound

Answers on page 122.

Lone Long Vowels

Some long vowels appear as single letters. The letters **i** and **o** can appear by themselves and still have the long vowel sound. Read the words on the left. Draw a line to match the word with its long vowel sound.

ghost

child

wild

gold

mild

roll

cold

Long **i**, like **kite**

Long **o**, like **boat**

Skill: Recognizing that some long vowel sounds, like long **i** and long **o**, can appear as single letters

26

Answers on page 122.

More Handy Dandy Words

Some handy words have long vowels. The long vowels appear at the end of the word. Say these handy dandy words out loud:

Long **e** sound: be he me she we
Long **o** sound: go no so hello

This child wants to be class president. Read the child's speech. Circle the correct missing handy dandy words.

(Hello) (We)!

I am happy to **(be, he)** here today.

(We, She) are having an election.

I hope you will vote for **(we, me)**.

When you **(go, so)** to vote, remember:

(No, So) matter what **(be, he)**

or **(she, me)** says about my kickball playing,

I can play kickball with the best of them!

(So, Be) vote for me on Election Day!

Parents: Help your child read the speech above. Review any difficult or unknown words. You might ask your child what he or she would say in a speech if they wanted to be elected class president.

Skill: Recognizing the long vowel sounds of **e** and **o** at the end of a word

Let's Go Camping!

Parents: Look through your home for objects that begin with the hard **c** sound, like cake, cookie, cup, counter, cat, curtain, and so on.

Skill: Recognizing the hard sound of the letter **c**

The letter **c** can make two different sounds. One sound is a hard sound, like the letter **k.** The word **camping** has a hard **c** sound. Look at the scene of the camping trip below. Say the words for the pictures you see. If the word begins with the hard **c** sound, circle the picture.

Answers on page 122.

City Sights

The letter **c** also makes a soft sound. The word **city** begins with the soft **c** sound. Look at the city in this picture. Say the word for each picture that has a write-on line. Write the letter **c** on the lines.

i ___ e

dan ___ e

mi ___ e

boun ___ e

___ elery

___ ircle

Skill: Recognizing the soft **c** sound

Answers on page 122.

Open the Gate!

The letter **g** can make two different sounds. One sound is a hard sound. The word **gate** has a hard **g** sound. Say the word for each picture. If the word begins with the hard **g** sound, circle the picture.

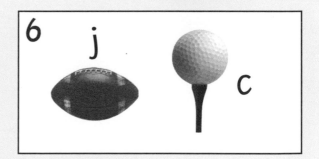

Now write the letters from the boxes you circled to reveal a secret word.

1.____ 2.____ 3.____ 4.____ 5.____ 6.____ **S** rocks!

Answers on page 122.

Going Soft

Now it's time to go soft! The letter **g** can also make a soft sound. The word **gym** begins with the soft **g** sound. Say the word for each picture. Write the letter **g** on the lines.

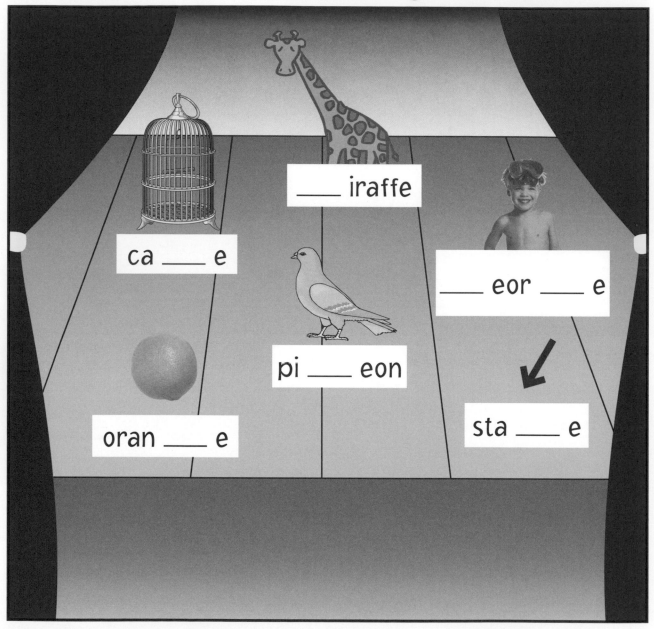

_____ iraffe

ca _____ e

pi _____ eon

_____ eor _____ e

oran _____ e

sta _____ e

Answers on page 122.

Skill Drill

When two consonants are at the beginning of a word, their sounds may be **blended.** These are called **consonant blends,** or **consonant clusters.** When you say the word **skill,** the **s** and the **k** are blended together. You can still hear both sounds, but you hear them at the same time. Read the words in each puzzle piece. Color the sections that contain the **sk-** sound blue.

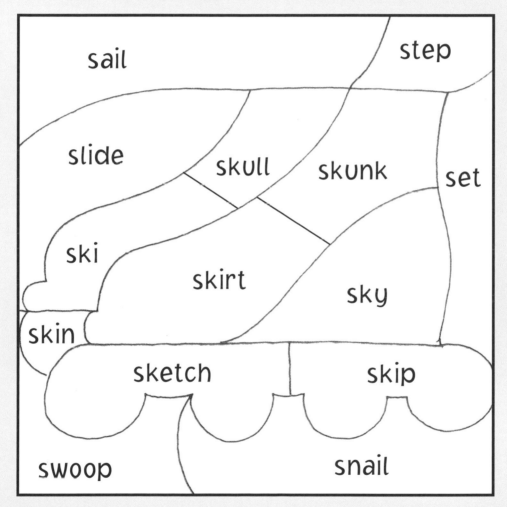

sail

step

slide

skull

skunk

set

ski

skirt

sky

skin

sketch

skip

swoop

snail

Parents: Ask your child to identify the picture revealed by coloring the sections containing **sk-** words. (A pair of skates.) Say the word with your child. Challenge your child to help you spell it, noticing the **sk-** sound, as well as the long **a** sound.

Skill: Recognizing the beginning consonant blend **sk-**

Answers on page 122.

Behind the Mask

When you say the word **desk,** the **s** and the **k** at the end of the word are blended together. You can still hear both letter sounds, but you hear them at the same time. Read each word in the masks below. Draw a star under the word that ends with the **-sk** sound.

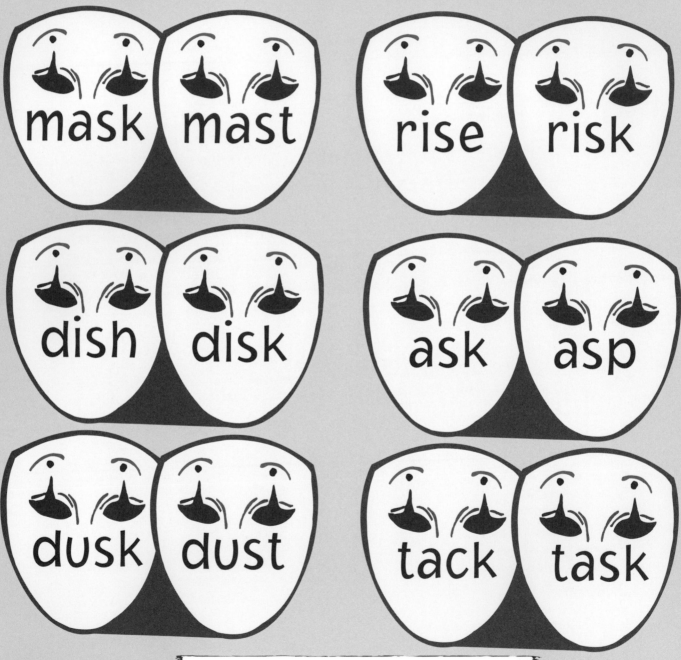

Answers on page 123.

Pizza Time!

When you say the word **sled,** the **s** and the **l** are blended together. You can still hear both sounds, but you hear them at the same time. Read the words in the pizza slices. Color in each pizza slice that has a word with the beginning **sl-** sound.

Answers on page 123.

Ready, Set, Smile!

When you say the word **smile,** the **s** and the **m** are blended together. You can still hear both sounds, but you hear them at the same time.

Read the words in the bursts. Color the bursts that have words with the **sm-** beginning consonant blend.

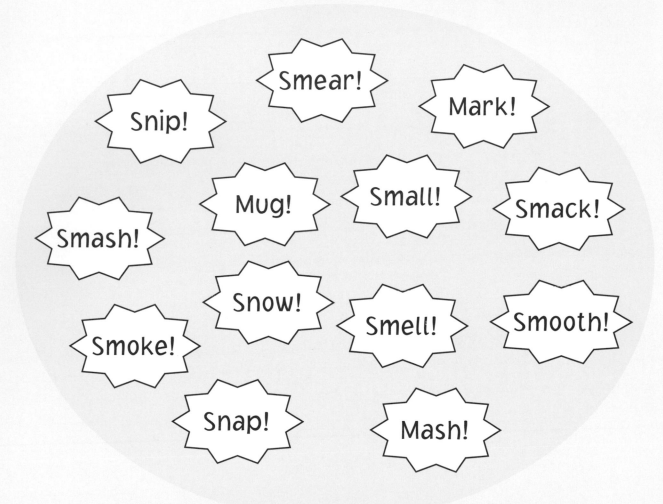

Parents: Point to the words that were not colored. Encourage your child to explain how the words differ from the **sm-** words. For example, three words begin with **sn-**. Three words do not have the beginning **s-** sound at all.

Skill: Recognizing the beginning consonant blend **sm-**

36

Answers on page 123.

Help, Please!

When you say the word **snag,** the **s** and the **n** are blended together. You can still hear both sounds, but you hear them at the same time.

Look at each picture. Say the word for each picture. Write the letters **sn-** to complete the word.

___ ___ eakers

___ ___ eeze

___ ___ ake

___ ___ ore

___ ___ ail

___ ___ ap

Skill: Recognizing the beginning consonant blend **sn-**

Answers on page 123.

Be a Spy!

When you say the word **spy,** the **s** and the **p** are blended together. You can still hear both sounds, but you hear them at the same time.

Find the words that begin with **sp-.** Look at the words in the magnifying glasses. Circle the words that begin with **sp-.**

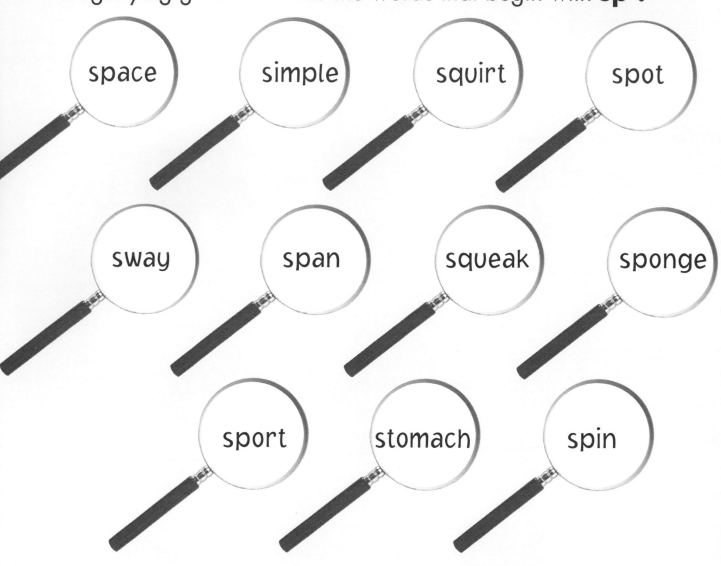

space   simple   squirt   spot

sway   span   squeak   sponge

sport   stomach   spin

Skill: Recognizing the beginning consonant blend **sp-**

Answers on page 123.

Star Power

When you say the word **star,** the **s** and the **t** are blended together. You can still hear both sounds, but you hear them at the same time.

Look at the picture in each star. Say the word for each picture. If you hear the **st-** sound at the beginning of the word, circle the star.

Skill: Recognizing the beginning consonant blend **st-**

Answers on page 123.

The Best Nest

When you say the word **nest,** the **s** and the **t** at the end of the word are blended together. You can still hear both letter sounds, but you hear them at the same time.

Read the words in the box. If the word ends with the blend **-st,** write the word in an egg in the bird's nest.

best	bird	farm	fast	ear	east
fin	first	much	must	pest	pet

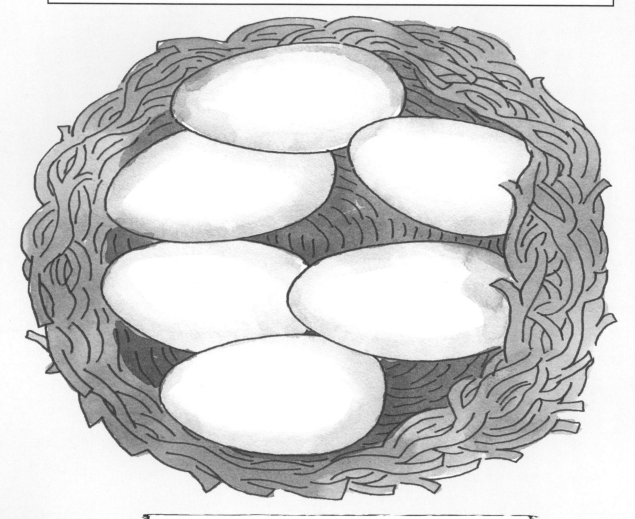

Skill: Recognizing the ending consonant blend **-st**

40

Answers on page 123.

Sweet!

When you say the word **sweet,** the **s** and the **w** are blended together. You can still hear both sounds, but you hear them at the same time.

Read each sentence. Complete the sentence with one of the **sw-** words from the box.

sweets	swan	sweater	sweeps	swims	swing

1. The white ___ ___ ___ ___ floats on the lake.

2. This warm ___ ___ ___ ___ ___ ___ ___ is itchy.

3. The ___ ___ ___ ___ ___ moves in the breeze.

4. Many people like to eat ___ ___ ___ ___ ___ ___ .

5. Jan ___ ___ ___ ___ ___ quickly.

6. Steve ___ ___ ___ ___ ___ the floor slowly.

Skill: Recognizing the beginning consonant blend **sw-**

Answers on page 123.

Color the Blanket

When you say the word **blend,** the **b** and the **l** are blended together. You can still hear both letter sounds, but you hear them at the same time.

Read the words on the blanket. Color the patches blue if they contain words with the **bl-** blend. (The word **blanket** has the **bl-** blend!)

blouse	beach	blaze
boom	black	barn
blow	book	blue
bank	block	back

Answers on page 123.

Flower Power!

When you say the word **floor,** the **f** and the **l** are blended together. You can still hear both letter sounds, but you hear them at the same time.

Find the hidden picture. Look at each word. If the word begins with the **fl-** blend, color that section yellow. If the word begins with the consonant **f,** color that section green. If the word begins with letters other than **fl-** or **f,** color that section blue.

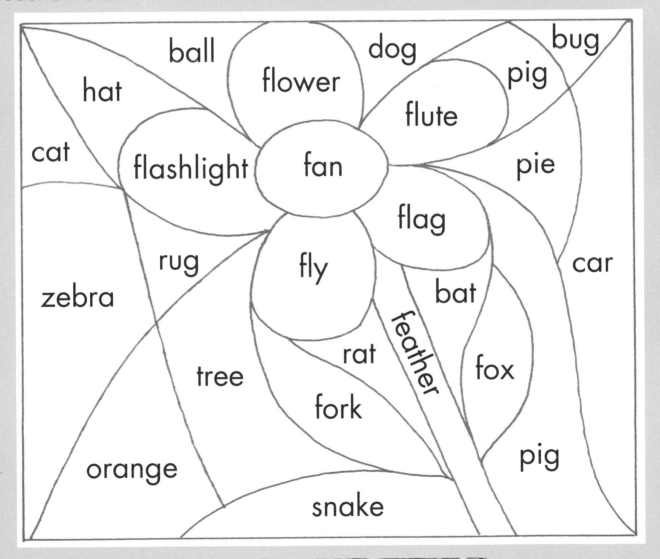

Skill: Recognizing the **fl-** consonant blend

Answers on page 123.

Click, Clack—You Can Spell That!

When you say the word **class,** the **c** and the **l** are blended together. You can still hear both letter sounds, but you hear them at the same time.

First, write the letter **c** at the beginning of each word below.

____ lean   ____ limb   ____ lass

Read the new words you made.

Write the letters **cl-** to complete each word. Now say the word for each picture.

____ ____ ock

____ ____ am

Parents: Point out that some **cl-** words are words that represent actual sounds. Say the word **click,** and have your child make a clicking sound. Say the word **cluck,** and ask your child which animal makes a clucking noise (a hen or chicken). Have your child make a clucking noise. Other sound words (or words of **onomatopoeia**) include **clack, clap, clang, clink,** and **clomp.**

Skill: Recognizing the **cl-** consonant blend

___ ___ ub

___ ___ aw

___ ___ oud

___ ___ own

___ ___ ip

___ ___ ap

Answers on page 123.

A Squirrel's Day

When you say the word **globe,** the **g** and the **l** are blended together. You can still hear both letter sounds, but you hear them at the same time. The squirrel keeps a journal. Read the squirrel's journal entry. Circle the words that start with **gl-.**

February 15

Last night, it snowed!
The snow glows in the morning sun.
The sun gleams off the snow.
The icy lake looks like glass.
The snow clings to tree branches.
It is like they are stuck there with glue!
I'm so glad it snowed!

Skill: Recognizing the **gl-** consonant blend

46

Answers on page 123.

Another Brick in the Wall

When you say the word **brick,** the **b** and the **r** are blended together. You can still hear both letter sounds, but you hear them at the same time.

This cat climbed up a brick wall, and now it cannot get back down. Help the cat climb down the wall. Find the words in the bricks that begin with the blend **br-.** Circle those bricks, from top to bottom, making a path down the wall.

brake	bed	read	eat
ground	brown	round	bow
room	boom	breath	snow
roar	brave	easy	rain
barn	rat	bridge	reach
father	sister	mother	brother

Skill: Recognizing the **br-** consonant blend

Answers on page 123.

Forecast: Cloudy!

When you say the word **please,** the **p** and the **l** are blended together. You can still hear both letter sounds, but you hear them at the same time.

Color the clouds with words with the **pl-** blend.

play

planet

paper

plenty

pencil

pig

puppy

plate

please

pet

plop

plane

plus

part

place

plant

plan

Answers on page 124.

Crop Busters

When you say the word **crop,** the **c** and the **r** are blended together. You can still hear both letter sounds, but you hear them at the same time.

Say the word for each picture. Write in the missing letters **cr-** at the beginning of each word.

__ __ ayon

__ __ own

__ __ y

__ __ icket

__ __ ib

__ __ ab

Skill: Recognizing the **cr-** consonant blend

50

Answers on page 124.

It's a Dream!

When you say the word **draw,** the **d** and the **r** are blended together. You can still hear both letter sounds, but you hear them at the same time.

The words in the box begin with **dr-.** Write the words in the spaces below. Some of the letters have been filled in for you.

draw   dress   drop   drum   dry

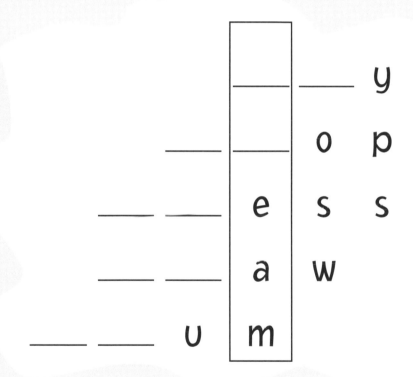

Now write the letters in the box.

——— ——— ——— ——— ———

Skill: Recognizing the **dr-** consonant blend

Answers on page 124.

A Frog's Delight

When you say the word **freckles,** the **f** and the **r** are blended together. You can still hear both letter sounds, but you hear them at the same time.

This frog can only hop on lily pads that have words with **fr-.** Help the frog get across the pond by drawing a path to each lily pad that has an **fr-** word.

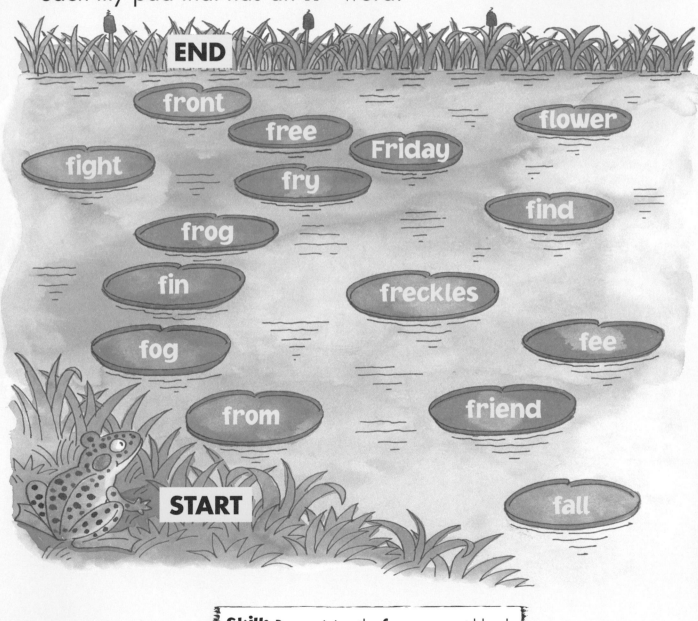

END

front

free

flower

Friday

fight

fry

find

frog

fin

freckles

fee

fog

friend

from

START

fall

Skill: Recognizing the **fr-** consonant blend

Answers on page 124.

A Great Gift

When you say the word **grab,** the **g** and the **r** are blended together. You can still hear both letter sounds, but you hear them at the same time.

Help this child complete a letter to his grandparents. Circle the words that begin with **gr-** in each space.

Dear (Grandma, Mom) and (Dad, Grandpa),

Thank you for my birthday gift!

How did you know I wanted a (goat, grasshopper)?

He is really (great, good)!

He is (green, red).

He likes to eat (cookies, grass)!

I wonder how big he will (get, grow)?

Your (grandson, girl),

(Greg, George)

Parents: Your child may write or dictate a letter to a grandparent, family member, or close friend. Tell your child to look and listen for words that begin with consonant blends, like **gr-**. Also point out that in this letter, the words **Grandma, Grandpa,** and **Greg** should begin with capital letters.

Skill: Recognizing the **gr-** consonant blend

The Prince's Prize

When you say the word **prop,** the **p** and the **r** are blended together. You can still hear both letter sounds, but you hear them at the same time.

Help this prince find the prize. (**Prince** and **prize** start with the blend **pr!**) Find the path with the words that begin with blend **pr-.** Follow the path until you reach the gold crown!

peach   peck

prove

promise   present

rain

ride   rice

Parents: Show your child a pretzel, a piece of fruit, and a nut. Ask your child to say the word for each food. Ask your child to identify which word begins with the **pr-** sound (**pretzel**).

Skill: Recognizing the **pr-** consonant blend

press

princess

pink

pretty

price

push

print

pop

pie

proud

practice

right

rent

raise

Answer on page 124.

It's Not a Trick!

When you say the word **trick,** the **t** and the **r** are blended together. You can still hear both letter sounds, but you hear them at the same time.

Say the word for the picture in each row. If you hear the **tr-** sound, write the letters **tr-** on the line. If you don't hear the **tr-** sound, leave the line blank.

56

Answers on page 124.

Twin Sets

When you say the word **twin,** the **t** and the **w** are blended together. You can still hear both letter sounds, but you hear them at the same time. Find the twin for each word and picture below.

Say the word for the picture on the left. Find the word that tells about that picture on the right. Draw a line to match the picture with the correct word. Also circle the letters **tw-** in each word.

twig

tweet

twins

twenty

twist

Skill: Recognizing the **tw-** consonant blend

Answers on page 124.

Check Out the Farm!

Sometimes two consonants at the beginning of a word make a new sound. When you say the word **check,** the **c** and the **h** make the **ch** sound, like in **chew.** The **ch** sound doesn't sound like **c** or **h.** It's something new.

Skill: Learning the sound of the consonant digraph **ch**

Say the word for the people, animals, and things on this farm. Use the words from the box to fill in the blanks.

children   chair   chickens
chase   chat   chicks

I Like Lunch!

The consonant digraph **ch** can also appear at the end of a word. Read the poem below about lunch. Write the missing letters **ch** on the lines.

I like lun ___ ___ !

It's su ___ ___ a fun treat.

I like to mun ___ ___ !

How mu ___ ___ can I eat?

I like to crun ___ ___ !

I tou ___ ___ and taste my food.

So let's eat lunch!
It's always good!

Skill: Recognizing the sound of the **ch** consonant digraph at the end of a word

60

Answers on page 124.

Shark!

Sometimes two consonants at the beginning of a word make a new sound. When you say the word **sheep,** the **s** and the **h** make the **sh** sound, like in **shoe.** The **sh** sound doesn't sound like **s** or **h.** It's something new.

Write the letters **sh** on the lines to complete each word.

We went on a **sh** ip.

I heard someone **sh** out.

sh e saw a **sh** ark under the water!

It had **sh** arp teeth.

Maybe it is safer to watch it from the **sh** ore!

There, we can look for **sh** ells.

Parents: Have your child look around the house for words that have the **sh** sound. Guide your child to identify these words: **shirt, shoe, dish, fish, shower, shovel, shampoo, shoelace, shorts,** and **shelf.** Encourage your child to draw a picture of each object, and help your child write the word.

Skill: Recognizing the sound of the **sh** consonant digraph

Answers on page 124.

Love Those Shoes!

a e i o u

Sometimes two consonants at the beginning of a word make a new sound. When you say the word **the,** the **t** and the **h** make the **th** sound. The **th** sound doesn't sound like **t** or **h.** It's something new. In **the,** the **th** sound is a bit harder than in some other words with **th,** like **think.**

Read the sentences below that tell about a girl's new shoes. Underline the words that begin with the letters **th.** Then circle the letters **th** in each word.

Do you like these shoes?

I bought them today!

They fit better than my old shoes.

I tried on that pair of shoes, too.

Then I tried on this pair.

They are the best shoes ever!

Skill: Recognizing the sound of the **th** consonant digraph

62

Answers on page 125.

Thanks a Lot!

Sometimes two consonants at the beginning of a word make a new sound. When you say the word **thank,** the **t** and the **h** make the **th** sound. The **th** sound doesn't sound like **t** or **h.** It's something new. In **thank,** the **th** sound is a bit softer than in some other words with **th,** like **the.** Say **thank** and **the.** Can you hear the difference in the **th** sound?

Say the word for each picture. Find the word in the box.

Write the word under the correct picture.

theater	thirteen	thirty	thumb	thimble	thread

theater

thirty

thumb

thread

thimble

thirteen

 Skill: Recognizing the voiceless or unvoiced sound of the **th** consonant digraph

The Lake Path

The consonant digraph **th** can also appear at the end of a word. Read the words in the lake. Circle the words that end with the letters **th** to get across the lake.

END

teeth

chick

month

fish

mouth

beach

flash

math

church

cloth

mush

bath

START

Skill: Recognizing the sound of the **th** consonant digraph at the end of a word

Answers on page 125.

A Wheelbarrow of Words

The consonant digraph **wh** is kind of tricky. When you say **wh,** it sounds like **hw.** Hold your hand up to your mouth, and say the word **whisper.** Can you feel your breath blowing against your hand? It is like when you say words that begin with the letter **h!**

Read each word. If the word begins with the consonant digraph **wh,** draw a line from the word to the wheelbarrow.

Answers on page 125.

Elephant Talk

Sometimes the letters **ph** make an **f** sound, like at the end of **graph.** Read the words below. Circle the letters **ph** in each word.

elephant

phone

photo

trophy

gopher

dolphin

Answers on page 125.

Rough Seas

Sometimes the letters **gh** make an **f** sound, like in the word **laugh.** Read each word below. Circle the words that make the **f** sound with the letters **gh.** Help the ship travel through rough seas by connecting the words you circled.

END

tug

dug

do

tough

touch

long

laugh

ride

rough

enough

egg

cough

ton

START

ocean

Parents: The next time you and your child laugh, write the word **laugh.** Ask your child to read it. Circle the **gh** in the word.

Skill: Recognizing the **gh** spelling pattern for the **f** sound

Meet the Knight!

Sometimes the letters **kn** are at the beginning of a word. In these words, the letter **k** is silent—you don't say it. You only say the **n** sound. The words **knight** and **know** have a silent **k** at the beginning. Read the story about this knight. Circle the words that begin with the letters **kn.** Underline the letters **kn,** too.

This is the story of one brave knight.

He was known across the land.

He knew how to ride a horse.

He could tie a knot.

He could also knit.

He was quite a knight!

Parents: Write words like **know, knuckle, knit,** and **knack,** but leave off the letters **kn** at the beginning. Have your child write in the letters **kn.** Look up other **kn** words in a picture dictionary.

Skill: Discovering that the letter **k** is silent when followed by the letter **n** at the beginning of a word

Answers on page 125.

Silent as a Secret Code

Sometimes the letters **wr** are at the beginning of a word. In these words, the letter **w** is silent—you don't say it. You only say the **r** sound. The word **wrench** has a silent **w** at the beginning.

Read each word. Circle the words that have a silent **w** at the beginning. Write the letters for the words you circled on the lines below.

1. whale   wreath   wind
   B   **G**   **R**

2. wrong   wink   wagon
   O   **A**   **L**

3. will   whistle   write
   Z   **M**   **O**

4. where   wrench   wizard
   E   **D**   **W**

5. wood   wheel   wrap
   H   **U**   **J**

6. wring   wing   whiff
   O   **T**   **C**

7. work   wrist   white
   n   **B**   **I**

Now write the letters that go with the words you circled, in order. This is the secret code!

____ ____ ____ ____   ____ ____ ____ !
1   2   3   4   5   6   7

Skill: Discovering that the letter **w** is silent when followed by the letter **r** at the beginning of a word

Answers on page 125.

Ar, Mateys!

Sometimes when you pair a vowel with the letter **r** you create a new sound. When you pair **a** with the letter **r,** you make the **ar** sound, like in **shark.** Pirates say the **ar** sound all the time! Help this pirate match the pictures with the correct **ar** words. Draw a line from the picture to the word.

Ar!

arm

barn

car

dart

jar

yarn

star

Skill: Recognizing the **ar** sound and spelling pattern

Answers on page 125.

The Clueless Clerk

Sometimes when you pair a vowel with the letter **r** you create a new sound. When you pair **e** with the letter **r,** you make the **er** sound, like at the end of **soccer.** This clerk is clueless! Help the clerk sort the cans on the shelves. Read each word. If you hear the **er** sound, color the can. (**Clerk** has the **er** sound and spelling!)

after desert did him her apple

camera team enter hat star person

Parents: Show your child examples of **er** words that you might have around your home. Talk about the meaning of each word, too. Then write the words, but omit the letters **er.** Have your child write in the letters **er** to complete each word.

Skill: Recognizing the **er** sound and spelling pattern

Answers on page 125.

nurse needs Help!

Sometimes when you pair a vowel with the letter **r** you create a new sound. When you pair **u** with the letter **r,** you make the **er** sound, like in **curl.** Help the nurse find her purse! Draw a line from the nurse through words that have the letters **ur** to lead her to her purse.

tub

hurt

smart

burn

large

turn

neat

curb

church

stir

fur

bank

hurl

dirt

urn

surprise

bun

skirt

Answers on page 125.

Digging in the Dirt

Sometimes when you pair a vowel with the letter **r** you create a new sound. When you pair **i** with the letter **r,** you make the **er** sound, like in **bird.** Read each word in the dirt. Color the letters **ir** yellow in each word.

Parents: Show your child that the letters **er, ur,** and **ir** make the same sound. It can be easy to misspell words with these letters. Write **ir** words on index cards. (Use the cards from the previous page and have your child sort the cards into **er, ur,** and **ir** piles.) The more your child is exposed to these words and spellings, the easier it will be for your child to recall the correct spelling in the future.

Skill: Recognizing the **ir** sound and spelling pattern

Answers on page 125.

Ready OR not!

Sometimes when you pair a vowel with the letter **r** you create a new sound. When you pair **o** with the letter **r,** you make the **or** sound, like in **horse.** Say the word for each picture and find the correct word in the box. Write the correct word below each picture.

corn   horn   acorn   fork   story

_____   _____   _____

_____   _____

Skill: Recognizing the **or** sound and spelling pattern

Answers on page 125.

Worm Work

The letters **or** can also make the **er** sound, like in **word**. Read the poem below. Write the letters **or** on the lines to complete each word.

I'm just a little w ___ ___ m,

Crawling in the dirt.

I have a special job,

I really like to w ___ ___ k.

I help our great big w ___ ___ ld,

By digging in the dirt.

I'm just a little w ___ ___ m,

But I know my own w ___ ___ th.

Parents: Have your child slip a sock over his or her hand and pretend the sock is a worm. Have your child recite the poem above, using the worm sock puppet. You might demonstrate first, exaggerating the **er** sound for each **or** word.

Skill: Learning that **or** can also make an **er** sound

Answers on page 125.

Do Your Laundry!

The letters **au** together make a sound like the **a** in **ball**. You can hear this sound in words like **haul** and **caught**.

Look at this pile of laundry. Color the clothes with words that have the letters **au**. (**Laundry** has the letters **au!**)

house · sense · brother · pause · Peter · August · cause · because · paint · daughter · faint · Paul

Skill: Recognizing the **au** sound and spelling pattern

Our House!

When you pair them, the letters **o** and **u** make a new sound. Together **ou** can make the **ou** sound, like in **cloud.** Read each word. Look for words that have the **ou** sound and the letters **ou.** Draw a line from each **ou** word to the house.

hound

cost

mouth

ground

moss

hint

count

mouse

Skill: Recognizing the **ou** sound and spelling pattern

Answers on page 126.

Words in a Haystack

Sometimes the letters **ay** make the long **a** sound, like in the word **hay.** Read the words in the haystack below. Circle the words that have the long **a** sound.

mat

day

climb

say

pat

clay

play

stay

saw

step

may

Parents: Read through a book or magazine with your child and look for words with the **ay** spelling pattern. Point out words and help your child read each one.

Skill: Recognizing the **ay** sound and spelling pattern

Answers on page 126.

Happy Birthday, Roy!

When you put them together, the letters **o** and **y** make a new sound. Together **oy** makes the **oi** sound, like in **boy.** Put the first letter and the letters **oy** together to make new words on the lines below.

1. b + oy = _____

2. j + oy = _____

3. t + oy = _____

4. R + oy = _____

Now use each word to fill in these sentences. The pictures will help you.

1. This is _____.

2. Roy has a new _____.

3. It gives Roy _____.

4. Roy is a happy _____.

Answers on page 126.

Aw, Shucks!

The letters **aw** together make the sound like in **law.**

Label the pictures on this page. Use the words from the box.

hawk   fawn   strawberry   paw   saw

Skill: Recognizing the **aw** sound and spelling pattern

Answers on page 126.

It's a Cow!

When you put them together, the letters **o** and **w** make a new sound. Together **ow** makes the **ou** sound, like in the word **down.** Look at each picture. The words below the pictures look almost the same, but they're not. One word is spelled incorrectly. Circle the words spelled with **ow.**

cow   cou

brown   broun

cloun   clown

frown   froun

town   toun

croun   crown

Parents: Ask your child to explain why the incorrect words are wrong. (They all have **ou** instead of **ow.**) Invite your child to write these words with the correct spellings.

Skill: Recognizing the **ow** spelling of the **ou** sound

Let It Snow!

The letters **ow** can also make the long **o** sound, like in **row**. Look at each picture. Read the words in the snowflakes. If the words have the long **o** sound, circle them.

crow

brow

row

mow

growl

howl

snow

grow

blow

cow

Build-a-Word

When you put them together, the letters **o** and **i** make a new sound. Together **oi** make the **oi** sound, like in **coin.** Build **oi** words by following the directions below.

1. Write the word **oil:** _____

2. Add the letter **c** to the beginning of **oil:** _____

3. Change the letter **l** to the letter **n:** _____

4. Change the letter **c** to the letter **j:** _____

5. Add the letter **t** to the end of the word: _____

6. Change the letter **j** to the letter **p:** _____

7. Change the letters **nt** to the letters **se:** _____

8. Change the letter **p** to the letter **n:** _____

Skill: Recognizing the **oi** sound and spelling pattern

Answers on page 126.

Ooo! Ooo! I Know the Answer!

The letters **oo** can make the long **u** sound, like you hear in the word **stool.** Say the word for each picture. Listen to the beginning and ending sounds. Draw a line to match the picture with the correct word.

boot

broom

goose

spoon

tooth

Skill: Recognizing the **oo** spelling of the long **u** sound

86

Answers on page 126.

Take a Look!

The letters **oo** can also make a different sound, like you hear in the word **good.** Take a look at the pictures below. Say the word for each item. Find the word in the box. Write the correct word under each picture.

| book | cook | foot | hood | hook | wood |

_____

_____

_____

_____

_____

_____

Skill: Recognizing that **oo** can make a different sound, like in **good**

Answers on page 126.

Shhh! Silent E

Some words end with the letter **e.** Sometimes this letter is silent. You do not say it. The letter **e** at the end of these words tells you that the other vowel in the word is a long vowel! Say the word for each picture. Circle the silent **e.** Then write the letter that makes the long vowel sound.

rake This word has the long _____ sound.

kite This word has the long _____ sound.

rope This word has the long _____ sound.

snake This word has the long _____ sound.

Parents: With your child, read a picture book or magazine article. Call attention to words with long vowel sounds that have silent **e** at the end. Write the words you find on a sheet of paper. Help your child pronounce each word, recognizing the silent **e** at the end of the word. Have your child circle the letter that makes the long vowel sound and underline the silent **e.**

Skill: Recognizing words with long vowel spelling patterns and silent **e**

Answers on page 126.

What Are We?

The letter **y** at the end of a word sometimes makes the long **e** sound, like in the word **berry.** Complete the labels to tell about the people and animals in the picture. Then answer the question at the bottom of the page.

Momm ___

Dadd ___

bab ___

kitt ___

pupp ___

Who are we? We are a famil __ !

Skill: Recognizing that the letter **y** at the end of a word can make a long **e** sound

Answers on page 126.

Follow the Butterfly!

The letter **y** at the end of a word sometimes makes the long **i** sound, like in **butterfly.** Help this butterfly get from one end of the garden to the other. Create a path by connecting the stones that have words with the long **i** sound and end with the letter **y.**

Skill: Recognizing that the letter **y** at the end of a word can make a long **i** sound

fly

fry

try

why

shy

hat

train

rain

fan

Answer on page 126.

Read All About It!

The letters **-all** make the sound you hear in the word **ball**. Fill in the blanks below with the letters from the box. Use each letter only once. Say the new words you make.

c   f   h   m   t   w

___ all   ___ all

___ all   ___ all

___ all   ___ all

Parents: Discuss the meanings of the words above. Then give your child a ball. Have your child say an **-all** word and pass the ball to you. Then say an **-all** word and pass the ball back to your child. Repeat this activity until you've reinforced the **-all** words from this page. Other words may include **all** and **small**.

Skill: Recognizing the **-all** sound and spelling pattern

Answers on page 126.

You Can Write It!

You can make many words with the letters **an.** These words have a short **a** sound and a consonant **n** sound. Look at the pictures and complete each word below with the letters **an.**

m _____ _____

v _____ _____

h _____ _____ d

c _____ _____

p _____ _____

f _____ _____

Answers on page 126.

That's It!

You can make words with the letters **-at.** These words have a short **a** sound and end with the consonant **t.** Look at each picture. Which beginning sound is missing? Use the letters in the box to write the missing beginning sound. You will only use each letter once.

b   c   h   m   r

____ at

____ at

____ at

____ at

____ at

Skill: Recognizing the **-at** sound and spelling

94

Answers on page 127.

Tell the Name

You can make words with the letters **-ell,** like the word **tell.** The **-ell** pattern uses a short **e** sound and the consonant sound **l.** Look at each picture and find the word in the box that matches. Write the words on the lines.

bell   shell   smell   well   yell

_____

_____

_____

_____

_____

Skill: Recognizing the **-ell** sound and spelling pattern

Answers on page 127.

Treasure Hunt

You can make words with the letters **-est,** like **vest.** The spelling pattern **-est** has the short **e** vowel sound and **-st** consonant blend. Help these kids find the treasure chest. Read the words in the sand below. Draw a line to connect the **-est** words to help the children reach the treasure chest.

tent

bead

west

test

START

part

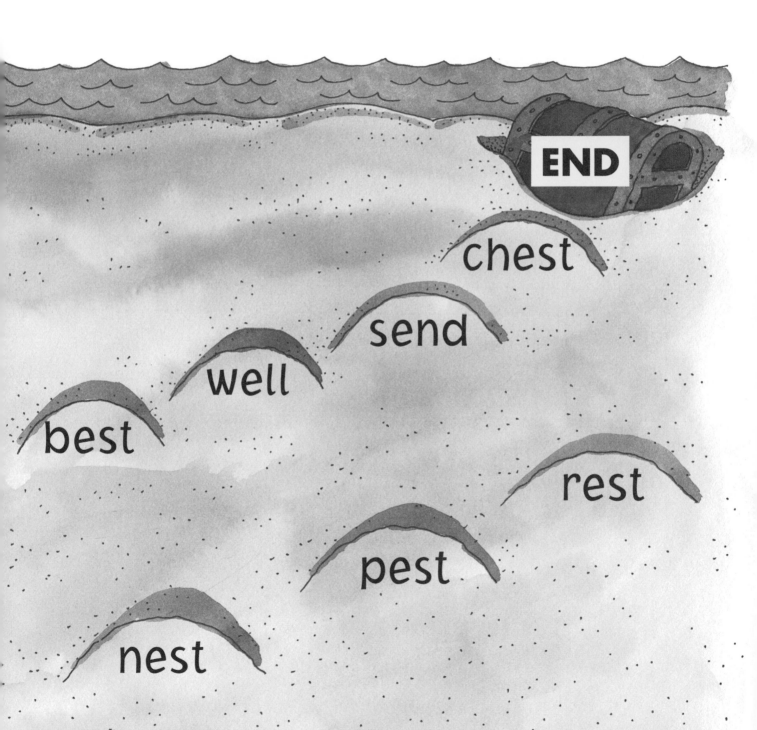

END

chest

send

well

best

rest

pest

nest

Answers on page 127.

Hidden Words

You can make words with the letters **-ide,** like **slide.** The letters **-ide** have the long **i** sound and the consonant sound **d.** The letter **e** is silent. You don't say it. Write the letters **-ide** to complete each word below. Read the words you've made.

sl _____

w _____

t _____

r _____

h _____

s _____

Parents: With your child, slide across the kitchen floor in your socks. Say these words as you do so: **We slide. We glide. We slide to the other side. We slide. We glide. We slide back to the other side.** Exaggerate the **-ide** sounds as you do so. Write the words **slide, glide,** and **side** on a sheet of paper. Have your child circle the letters **-ide** in each word.

Skill: Recognizing the **-ide** sound and spelling pattern

Answers on page 127.

Contraction Action

Sometimes you can put two words together using an apostrophe. These words are called **contractions.** When you form a contraction, some letters are left out. For example: **I am** becomes **I'm. You are** becomes **you're.** Say each word pair. Draw a line to the contraction it forms.

do not	**here's**
is not	**don't**
I have	**we're**
we are	**isn't**
here is	**couldn't**
they are	**I've**
could not	**they're**

Answers on page 127.

A Web of Words

You can make words with the letters **-ing,** like **string.** The letters **-ing** have the short **i** sound and the final consonant blend **-ng.** Read the words. Draw a string from the word **string** in the center to words with the **-ing** spelling pattern.

sing

bring

swing

back

string

ring

swim

was

king

wing

sign

Answers on page 127.

Let's Skate!

You can make words with the letters **-ink,** like **rink.** The letters **-ink** have the short **i** sound and the final consonant blend **-nk.** Read each word in the skating rink. Circle the letters **-ink** in each word.

link
pink
drink
stink
wink
blink
sink
think

Skill: Recognizing the **-ink** sound and spelling pattern

Answers on page 127.

Between a Rock and a Hard Place

You can make words with the letters **-ock,** like **clock.** The letter **o** makes the short **o** sound. The letters **ck** make the hard **k** sound. Practice writing **-ock** words by following the directions. The pictures will help you.

 1. Write the letter **r:** _____ ock

 2. Change the **r** to a **d:** _____ ock

 3. Change the **d** to an **s:** _____ ock

 4. Change the **s** to an **l:** _____ ock

 5. Add the letter **c** to the beginning: _____ lock

 6. Change the **c** to a **b:** _____ lock

Skill: Recognizing the **-ock** sound and spelling pattern

102

Answers on page 127.

Hop to It!

You can make words with the letters **-op,** like **mop.** The letter **o** makes the short **o** sound. The letter **p** makes the consonant sound **p.** Help the rabbit hop to its den. Circle the words in the meadow that have the **-op** sound. Connect the words you've circled to lead the rabbit to its den.

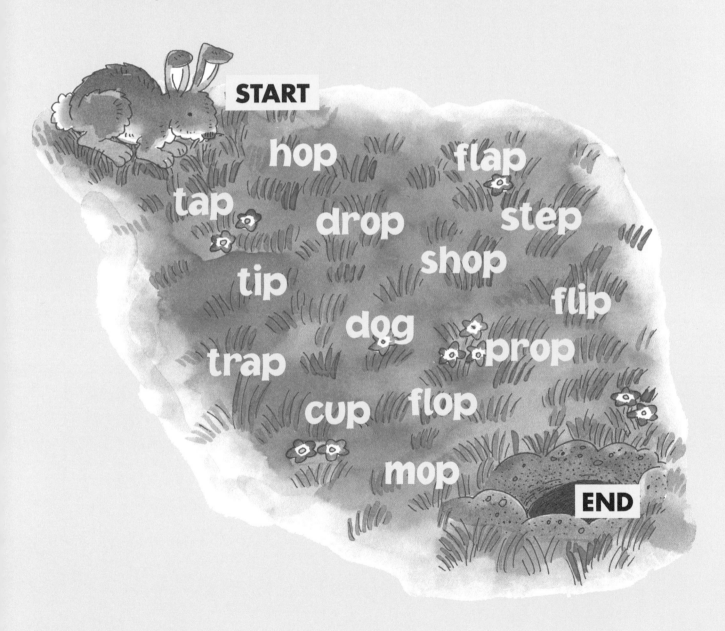

START

hop   flap

tap   drop   step

shop

tip   flip

dog   prop

trap

cup   flop

mop

END

Pour It in the Mug!

You can make words with the letters **-ug,** like **bug.** The letter **u** makes the short **u** sound. The letter **g** makes the hard **g** sound. Look at the letters in the mug. Add **-ug** after each letter to make a word.

t ___ ___

h ___ ___

d ___ ___

m ___ ___

j ___ ___

r ___ ___

Parents: Work with your child to come up with additional words that have the **-ug** spelling pattern. Along with the words on this page, you and your child can write and read **lug, pug, slug, snug,** and **shrug.**

Skill: Recognizing the **-ug** sound and spelling pattern

104

Answers on page 127.

What Is It?

You can make words with the letters **-unk,** like **junk.** The letter **u** makes the short **u** sound. The letters **nk** make the final consonant blend **nk.** Read each riddle. Answer each riddle with a word from the box.

| bunk | junk | sunk | trunk | skunk |

1. What the leaky boat did.   __ __ __ __

2. What is a lot of useless stuff?   __ __ __ __

3. What animal can make a bad smell?   __ __ __ __ __

4. You put stuff in this.   __ __ __ __ __

5. You might sleep in the top or bottom one.   __ __ __ __

A Pirate's Treasure

Most words are made plural by adding the letter **-s** to the end of the word.

1 pirate | **2 pirates**

1 parrot | **2 parrots**

Write the letter **-s** on the end of the word if it should be plural.

coin _____ | coin _____

cow _____ | cow _____

crown _____ | crown _____

ring _____ | ring _____

car _____ | car _____

hat _____ | hat _____

Answers on page 127.

More than One Way

Some words are made plural by adding the letters **-es** to the end of the word.

1 dish | **2 dishes**

1 lunch | **2 lunches**

Look at the pictures. Circle the plural form of the word.

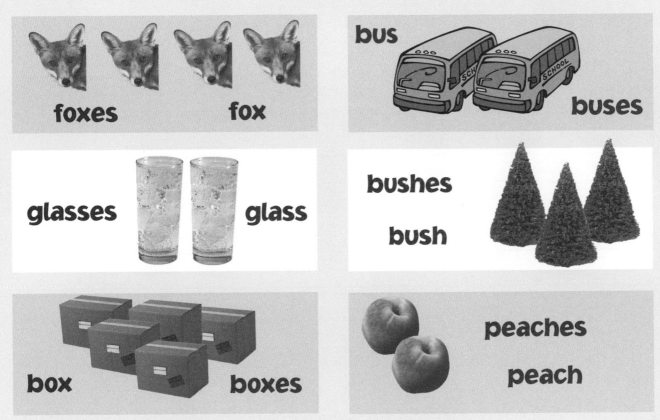

foxes   fox

bus   buses

glasses   glass

bushes   bush

box   boxes

peaches   peach

Parents: Write each of the words on this page on a sheet of paper. Leave off the plural **-es.** Ask your child to write the **-es** to make each word plural. Other words you could introduce to your child include **beaches, classes,** and **benches.**

Skill: Adding **-es** to words to make them plural

Answers on page 127.

It's Not Normal!

You already know how to make plural words by adding **-s** and **-es.** Some words change in different ways to make the plural form. Read the word under each picture and pick the correct plural from the box. Write the plural on the line under the picture.

feet   people   men   mice
children   teeth   geese

child _____   man _____

person _____

tooth _____

goose _____

mouse _____

foot _____

Skill: Recognizing irregular plurals

Answers on page 128.

Drop the Y!

Words that end in **y** are made plural by changing the **y** to an **i** and adding the letters **-es.** So one **penny** becomes five **pennies.**

 1 penny

 5 pennies

Look at the pictures and circle the word that matches what you see.

 daisy

daisies

 baby

babies

 puppy

puppies

 berry

berries

What else do these words have in common? They all end in **y,** and the letter **y** comes after a consonant! So if you see a consonant and **y,** the word is probably made plural by changing the **y** to an **i** and adding **-es.**

Answers on page 128.

Look What I Am Doing!

Adding the letters **-ing** to the end of a word makes the word **present tense.** The word tells about something that is happening now. For example:

| I **talk** to my teacher. | I am **talking** to my teacher now. |

Look at what each cat is doing. Circle the word in each sentence that has the letters **-ing.**

The cat is sleeping.

I am talking on the phone.

I am cooking soup.

The cat is painting a picture.

She is playing with the yarn.

Skill: Recognizing present tense words with **-ing**

Answers on page 128.

What the Lion Did

Adding the letters **-ed** to the end of a word makes the word **past tense.** Past tense means that a word tells about something that was done before, or in the past.

For example:

Today I **talk** to my teacher.

Yesterday I **talked** to my teacher.

Tell what the lion did. Add the letters **-ed** to each action word.

roar ___ ___

jump ___ ___

cover ___ ___

walk ___ ___

splash ___ ___

Skill: Learning to write the past tense by adding **-ed**

Answers on page 128.

Who Is the Most?

Adding the letters **-est** to the end of a word makes the word mean **the most.** Adding the letters **-est** helps compare two or more things.

It is **cold** outside.   It is the **coldest** day of the year!

Look at the fans at this football game. Label each fan to tell about him or her. Use the words in the box.

loudest   saddest   tallest   youngest

Skill: Comparing two or more things by adding **-est** to adjectives

Answers on page 128.

Who Is More?

Adding the letters **-er** to the end of a word can make the word mean **more.** Adding the letters **-er** helps people compare two things.

This school is **small.**   Our school is **smaller.**

Read about these animals. Circle the word that best compares the animals.

The turtle is (slow, slower) than the cat.

The cat is (softer, soft) than the turtle.

The elepaht is (stronger, strong) than the goose.

The goose is (small, smaller) than the elephant.

Skill: Comparing two things by adding **-er** to adjectives

Answers on page 128.

Double Up!

Sometimes you need to double the last letter of a word if you add a suffix. For example:

hot   hotter   hottest

Rewrite these words by doubling the last letter and adding **-ed.**

stop _____   hop _____

Rewrite these words by doubling the last letter and adding **-ing.**

run _____   tug _____

Rewrite these words by doubling the last letter and adding **-est.**

wet _____   sad _____

Skill: Doubling the last consonant when a suffix is added

Answers on page 128.

Syllable Sounds

A **syllable** is the sound contained in a part of a word. Some words only have one syllable. Words like **run, go, my, to, bike,** and **dog** have only one syllable. Some words have two syllables. The words have two parts. **Window** has two parts: **win•dow. Giraffe** also has two parts: **gir•affe.** Read the words in the picture. If the word has **one** syllable, color the section green. If the word has **two** syllables, color the section orange.

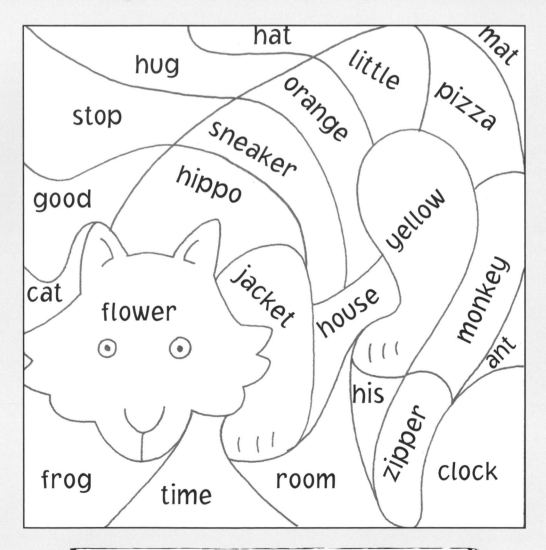

Skill: Counting syllables in one- and two-syllable words

Answers on page 128.

Splitting Syllables

Words with more than one syllable can be long words. Dividing long words into syllables can help you read them. If you see two consonants in the middle of a word, you can often divide the word between those two letters, like **rabbit: rab•bit.** Read the word for each picture. Draw a line down the middle of the word to show the syllables.

bubble

turkey

pizza

monkey

raccoon

kitten

Bonus:

How many syllables do the words above have? _____

Skill: Dividing words into syllables

Put Them Together

Some words are made up of two words. These words are called **compound words.** Put the two words together to make a compound word.

foot + ball = _____

light + house = _____

grand + mother = _____

cow + boy = _____

gold + fish = _____

bath + tub = _____

skate + board = _____

air + port = _____

bull + frog = _____

pop + corn = _____

Parents: Write compound words on index cards. Use the words on these two pages. Other compound words include **doghouse, flowerpot, bookshelf, bedroom,** and **dishwasher.** Cut the cards in half, separating each individual word. Have your child put the cards back together to make the compound words.

Skill: Creating compound words

Answers on page 128.

Working with Words

Use everything you have learned about phonics to read the following poem. It's about reading and phonics. Circle the words that rhyme.

Working with words can be lots of fun.

Phonics helps me read words by the ton.

The world is full of words, so many to know.

Words to help me learn and grow.

With reading I can learn about lots of stuff.

There's so much to read. I can't read enough!

I know reading will show me the way.

And my reading will grow every day.

Hooray! You've completed this book about reading and phonics! Write your name on the line and read the message!

_____

IS GREAT AT PHONICS!

Parents: Continue working with your child to build knowledge of letter-sound relationships. Provide a variety of reading materials so your child has plenty of opportunities to practice reading skills.

Skill: Using a variety of phonics concepts to read

Answers on page 128.

Answer Pages

page 7

page 8

page 9

page 10

page 11

page 12

page 13

page 14

page 15

page 16

page 17

page 18

page 19

Jump on the Bus!

The letter **u** can make the short **u** sound, like in **bus**. Only words with the short **u** sound can get the bus to school. Which words are they? Say the words on the path. Draw a line to follow the words with short **u** sounds.

leaf · tree · tree · ball · shoe · plant · can · trap · log · rat · dog · two · tall · slant · log

page 20

Rain, Rain, Go Away!

The letter **a** can make the long **a** sound, like in **rain**. Say the word in each raindrop. If you hear the long **a**, color the raindrop blue. If you don't hear the long **a**, draw an **X** through the raindrop.

rake · lamp · snake · apple · train · door · cake · gate · cat · brain

page 21

Feel the Beat!

The letter **e** can make the long **e** sound, like in **feel** and **beat**. Say the word for each picture. In each space, write in the missing letter **e**.

e_agle · tr_e_e · qu_e_e_n · b_e_agle · f_e_e_t · j_e_ans · s_e_at

page 22

Oh, No!

The letter **o** can make the long **o** sound, like in **oat**. Say the words for these pictures. Circle the pictures with long **o** sounds.

page 23

page 24

The I's Have It!

The letter **i** can make the long **i** sound, like in **hive**. Say the name of each picture in the row. If the word has the long **i** sound, circle the picture.

4 5 6
7 8 9

page 25

Unicorns Know Best

The letter **u** can make the long **u** sound, like in **unicorn**. Say the words for these pictures. Circle the correct long **u** word for each picture.

cube / cub · tub / tube · blue / bell · glob / glue · foot / fruit · suit / sit

page 26

Lone Long Vowels

Some long vowels appear as single letters. The letters **i** and **o** can appear by themselves and still have the long vowel sound. Read the words on the left. Draw a line to match the word with its long vowel sound.

ghost · child · wild · gold · mild · roll · cold

Long i, like **kite**
Long o, like **boat**

page 27

More Handy Dandy Words

Some handy words have long vowels. The long vowels appear at the end of the word. Say these handy dandy words out loud:

Long **e** sound: be he me she we
Long **o** sound: go no so hello

This child wants to be class president. Read the child's speech. Circle the correct missing handy dandy words.

Hello / We!
I am happy to (be / he) here today.
(We / She) are having an election.
I hope you will vote for (we / me).
When you (go / so) to vote, remember:
(No / so) matter what (be / he)
or (she / me) says about my kickball playing,
I can play kickball with the best of them!
(So / Be) vote for me on Election Day!

page 28

Let's Go Camping!

page 29

The letter **c** can make two different sounds. One sound is a hard sound, like the letter **k**. The word **camping** has a hard **c** sound. Look at the scene of the camping trip below. Say the words for the pictures you see. If the word begins with the hard **c** sound, circle the picture.

page 30

City Sights

The letter **c** also makes a soft sound. The word **city** begins with the soft **c** sound. Look at the city in this picture. Say the word for each picture that has a write-on line. Write the letter **c** on the lines.

i _c_ e · dan _c_ e · mi _c_ e · boun _c_ e · _c_ eteru · _c_ ircle

page 31

Open the Gate!

The letter **g** can make two different sounds. One sound is a hard sound. The word **gate** has a hard **g** sound. Say the word for each picture. If the word begins with the hard **g** sound, circle the picture.

1 H p · 2 h L · 3 B o · 4 z n · 5 i u · 6 j c

Now write the letters from the boxes you circled to reveal a secret word.

P H O N I C S rocks!
1 2 3 4 5 6 7

page 32

Going Soft

Now it's time to go soft! The letter **g** can also make a soft sound. The word **gym** begins with the soft **g** sound. Say the word for each picture. Write the letter **g** on the lines.

g_iraffe · ca_g_e · G_eor_g_e · pi_g_eon · sta_g_e · oran_g_e

page 33

Skill Drill

When two consonants are at the beginning of a word, their sounds may be **blended**. These are called **consonant blends**, or **consonant clusters**. When you say the word **skill**, the **s** and the **k** are blended together. You can still hear both sounds, but you hear them at the same time. Read the words in each puzzle piece. Color the sections that contain the **sk-** sound blue.

sail · step · slide · skill · skunk · set · ski · skirt · sky · sketch · skip · swoop · snail

page 34

Behind the Mask

When you say the word **desk**, the **s** and the **k** at the end of the word are blended together. You can still hear both sounds, but you hear them at the same time. Read each word in the masks below. Draw a star under the word that ends with the **-sk** sound.

mask ★ / mast — rise / risk ★
dish / disk ★ — ask ★ / asp
dusk ★ / dust — tack / task ★

SKILL: Recognizing the ending consonant blend sk

Answers on page 123.

page 35

Pizza Time!

When you say the word **sled**, the **s** and the **l** are blended together. You can still hear both sounds, but you hear them at the same time. Read the words in the pizza slices. Color in each pizza slice that has a word with the beginning **sl-** sound.

sleep / slug / sun
stam / sock / slime
steam / sleeve / slipper

SKILL: Recognizing the beginning consonant blend sl-

Answers on page 123.

page 36

Ready, Set, Smile!

When you say the word **smile**, the **s** and the **m** are blended together. You can still hear both sounds, but you hear them at the same time.

Read the words in the bursts. Color the bursts that have words with the **sm-** beginning consonant blend.

Snip! / Smear! / Mark!
Smash! / Mug! / Small! / Smack!
Smoke! / Snow! / Smile! / Smooth!
Snap! / Mash!

Parents: ...

SKILL: Recognizing the beginning consonant blend sm-

Answers on page 123.

page 37

Help, Please!

When you say the word **snag**, the **s** and the **n** are blended together. You can still hear both sounds, but you hear them at the same time.

Look at each picture. Say the word for each picture. Write the letters **sn-** to complete the word.

sneakers — **sn**eeze — **sn**ake
snore — **sn**ail — **sn**ap

SKILL: Recognizing the beginning consonant blend sn-

Answers on page 123.

page 38

Be a Spy!

When you say the word **spy**, the **s** and the **p** are blended together. You can still hear both sounds, but you hear them at the same time.

Find the words that begin with **sp-**. Look at the words in the magnifying glasses. Circle the words that begin with **sp-**.

space / simple / squirt / spot
sway / span / squeak / sponge
spot / stomach / skin

SKILL: Recognizing the beginning consonant blend sp-

Answers on page 123.

page 39

Star Power

When you say the word **star**, the **s** and the **t** at the end of the word are blended together. You can still hear both sounds, but you hear them at the same time.

Look at the picture in each star. Say the word for each picture. If you hear the **st-** sound at the beginning of the word, circle the star.

SKILL: Recognizing the beginning consonant blend st-

Answers on page 123.

page 40

The Best Nest

When you say the word **nest**, the **s** and the **t** at the end of the word are blended together. You can still hear both letter sounds, but you hear them at the same time.

Read the words in the box. If the word ends with the blend **-st**, write the word in an egg in the bird's nest.

best bird farm fast ear east
fin first much must pest pet

best / fast / east / first / pest / must

SKILL: Recognizing the ending consonant blend st

Answers on page 123.

page 41

Sweet!

When you say the word **sweet**, the **s** and the **w** are blended together. You can still hear both sounds, but you hear them at the same time.

Read each sentence. Complete the sentence with one of the **sw-** words from the box.

sweets swan sweater sweeps swims swing

1. The white **swan** floats on the lake.
2. This warm **sweater** is itchy.
3. The **swing** moves in the breeze.
4. Many people like to eat **sweets**.
5. Jan **swims** quickly.
6. Steve **sweeps** the floor slowly.

SKILL: Recognizing the beginning consonant blend sw-

Answers on page 123.

page 42

Color the Blanket

When you say the word **blend**, the **b** and the **l** are blended together. You can still hear both letter sounds, but you hear them at the same time.

Read the words on the blanket. Color the patches blue if they contain words with the **bl-** blend. (The word **blanket** has the **bl-** blend!)

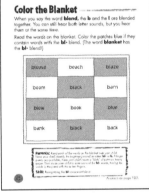

blouse	beach	blaze
boom	black	barn
blow	book	blue
bank	block	back

Parents: ...

SKILL: Recognizing the bl- consonant blend

Answers on page 123.

page 43

Flower Power!

When you say the word **floor**, the **f** and the **l** are blended together. You can still hear both letter sounds, but you hear them at the same time.

Find the hidden picture. Look at each word. If the word begins with the **fl-** blend, color that section yellow. If the word begins with the consonant **f**, color that section green. If the word begins with letters other than **fl-** or **f**, color that section blue.

ball / dog / bug / hat / flower / flute / pig / cat / flashlight / fan / pie / zebra / flag / car / rug / fly / bat / tree / rat / fox / orange / fork / pig / snake

SKILL: Recognizing the fl- consonant blend

Answers on page 123.

page 44

Click, Clack—You Can Spell That!

When you say the word **class**, the **c** and the **l** are blended together. You can still hear both letter sounds, but you hear them at the same time.

First, write the letter **c** at the beginning of each word below.

clean **c**limb **c**lass

Read the new words you made.

Write the letters **cl-** to complete each word. Now say the word for each picture.

clock — **cl**am
club — **cl**aw
cloud — **cl**own
clip — **cl**ap

Parents: ...

SKILL: Recognizing the cl- consonant blend

Answers on page 123.

page 45

(see page 44)

page 46

A Squirrel's Day

When you say the word **globe**, the **g** and the **l** are blended together. You can still hear both letter sounds, but you hear them at the same time. The squirrel keeps a journal. Read the squirrel's journal entry. Circle the words that start with **gl-**.

February 15

Last night, it snowed!
The snow glows in the morning sun.
The sun gleams off the snow.
The icy lake looks like glass.
The snow clings to tree branches.
It is like they are stuck there with glue.
I'm so glad it snowed!

SKILL: Recognizing the gl- consonant blend

Answers on page 123.

page 47

Another Brick in the Wall

When you say the word **brick**, the **b** and the **r** are blended together. You can still hear both letter sounds, but you hear them at the same time.

This cat climbed up a brick wall, and now it cannot get back down. Help the cat climb down the wall. Find the words in the bricks that begin with **br-**. Circle those bricks, from top to bottom, making a path down the wall.

brake / bed / read / eel
around / brown / round / bow
room / boom / breathe / snow
roar / brave / easy / rain
barn / rat / bridge / reach
father / sister / mother / brother

SKILL: Recognizing the br- consonant blend

Answers on page 123.

page 48   page 49

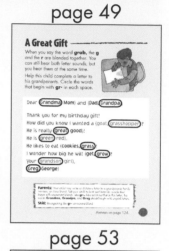

page 50   page 51   page 52   page 53

page 54   page 55   page 56   page 57

page 58   page 59   page 60   page 61

Love Those Shoes!

Do you like these shoes?

I bought them today!

They fit better than my old shoes.

I tried on that pair of shoes, too.

Then I tried on this pair.

They are the best shoes ever!

page 62

Thanks a Lot!

theater thirteen thirty thumb thimble thread

 30 — thirty
thumb
theater
thread
thimble
13 — thirteen

page 63

The Lake Path

END
teeth   chick
month   fish
mouth   beach
flash   math   church
cloth   mush
bath
START

page 64

A Wheelbarrow of Words

wheat   cup   wheel   lion   white
pig   socks   whistle
van
whale

page 65

Elephant Talk

elephant   phone   photo
trophy   gopher   dolphin

page 66

Rough Seas

END
do   tough   lug   dug
long   touch
ride   laugh
enough   rough
egg
cough
tan
ocean   START

page 67

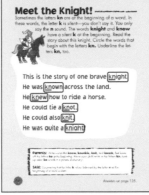

Meet the Knight!

This is the story of one brave knight

He was known across the land.

He knew how to ride a horse.

He could tie a knot.

He could also knit.

He was quite a knight.

page 68

Silent as a Secret Code

1. whale wreath wind   B G R
2. wrong wink wagon   O A L
3. wilt whistle write   Z M O
4. where wrench wizard   E D W
5. wood wind wrap   H U J
6. wring wing whiff   O I N
7. work wrist white   D B I

g o o d   j o b
1 2 3 4   5 6 7

page 69

Ar, Mateys!

arm
barn
car
dart
jar
yarn
star

page 70

The Clueless Clerk

alter   desert   did   him   her   apple

camera   team   enter   hat   star   other

page 71

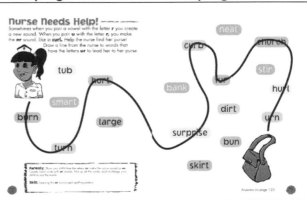

Nurse Needs Help!

neat
curb   church
stir
tub   hurt   fur
bank   hurl
smart   dirt
born   urn
large
surprise   bun
turn   skirt

page 72

Digging in the Dirt

dirt
bird   stir
first   skirt
third
shirt

page 74

Ready OR Not!

corn horn acorn fork story

corn   horn   fork
story   acorn

page 75

Worm Work

I'm just a little w o r m,

Crawling in the dirt.

I have a special job,

I really like to w o r k.

I help our great big w o r ld,

By digging in the dirt.

I'm just a little w o r m,

But I know my own w o r th.

page 76

Do Your Laundry!

house   sense   gopher   pause
cause
Peter   because
laughter   paint
faint   Paul

page 77

Our House!
When you pair them, the letters **o** and **u** make a new sound. Together **ou** can make the **ou** sound, like in **cloud**. Read each word. Look for words that have the **ou** sound and the letters **ou**. Draw a line from each **ou** word to the house.

hound — cost — mouth
ground — moss
hint — count
mouse

Skill: Learning the **ou** sound and spelling pattern

page 78

Words in a Haystack
Sometimes the letters **ay** make the long **a** sound, like in the word **hay**. Read the words in the haystack below. Circle the words that have the long **a** sound.

mat, day, climb, pat, clay, say, play, stay, saw, step, may

Parents: ...
Skill: Recognizing the **ay** sound and spelling pattern

page 79

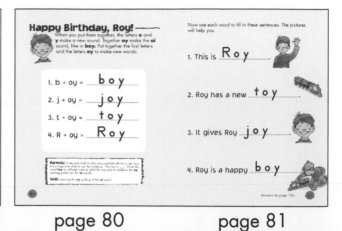

Happy Birthday, Roy!
When you put them together, the letters **o** and **y** make a new sound. Together **oy** make the **oi** sound, like in **boy**. Put together the first letters and the letters **oy** to make new words.

1. b + oy = **b o y**
2. j + oy = **j o y**
3. t + oy = **t o y**
4. R + oy = **R o y**

Now use each word to fill in these sentences. The pictures will help you.

1. This is **R o y**
2. Roy has a new **t o y**
3. It gives Roy **j o y**
4. Roy is a happy **b o y**

Parents: ...
Skill: Learning the **oy** spelling of the **oi** sound

page 80

page 81

Aw, Shucks!
The letters **aw** together make the sound like in **law**. Label the pictures on this page. Use the words from the box.

hawk   fawn   strawberry   paw   saw

hawk
fawn
paw
saw
strawberry

Skill: Recognizing the **aw** sound and spelling pattern

page 82

It's a Cow!
When you put them together, the letters **o** and **w** make a new sound. Together **ow** make the **ou** sound, like in the word **down**. Look at each picture. The words below the pictures look almost the same, but they're not. One word is spelled incorrectly. Circle the words spelled with **ow**.

cow   cou
brown   broun
ctoun   clown
frown   troun
town   toun
croun   crown

Parents: ...
Skill: Recognizing the **ow** spelling of the **ou** sound

page 83

Let It Snow!
The letters **ow** can also make the long **o** sound, like in **row**. Look at each picture. Read the words in the snowflakes. If the words have the long **o** sound, circle them.

crow   brow   row
mow   growl
howl   snow   grow
blow   cow

Skill: Recognizing the **ow** spelling of the long **o** sound

page 84

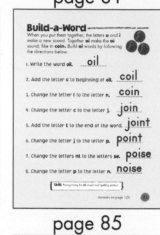

Build-a-Word
When you put them together, the letters **o** and **i** make a new sound, like in **coin**. Together **oi** make the **oi** sound. Build **oi** words by following the directions below.

1. Write the word **oil**.   **oil**
2. Add the letter **c** to beginning of **oil**.   **coil**
3. Change the letter **l** to the letter **n**.   **coin**
4. Change the letter **c** to the letter **j**.   **join**
5. Add the letter **t** to the end of the word.   **joint**
6. Change the letter **j** to the letter **p**.   **point**
7. Change the letters **nt** to the letters **se**.   **poise**
8. Change the letter **p** to the letter **n**.   **noise**

Skill: Recognizing the **oi** sound and spelling pattern

page 85

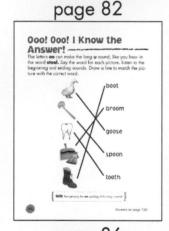

Ooo! Ooo! I Know the Answer!
The letters **oo** can make the long **u** sound, like you hear in the word **stool**. Say the word for each picture. Listen to the beginning and ending sounds. Draw a line to match the picture with the correct word.

boot
broom
goose
spoon
tooth

Skill: Recognizing the **oo** spelling of the long **u** sound

page 86

Take a Look!
The letters **oo** can also make a different sound, like you hear in the word **good**. Take a look at the pictures below. Say the word for each item. Find the word in the box. Write the correct word under each picture.

book   cook   foot   hood   hook   wood

wood   hook   foot
book   cook   hood

Skill: Recognizing the **oo** sound in **good**

page 87

Shhh! Silent E
Some words end with the letter **e**. Sometimes this letter is silent. You do not say it. The letter **e** at the end of these words tells you that the other vowel in the word is a long vowel. Say the word for each picture. Circle the silent **e**. Then write the letter that tells the long vowel sound.

rake — This word has the long **a** sound.
kite — This word has the long **i** sound.
rope — This word has the long **o** sound.
snake — This word has the long **a** sound.

Parents: ...
Skill: Recognizing words with long vowel spelling patterns and silent e

page 88

What Are We?
The letter **y** at the end of a word sometimes makes the long **e** sound, like in the word **berry**. Complete the labels to tell about the people and animals in the picture. Then answer the question at the bottom of the page.

Momm**y**
Dadd**y**   bab**y**
kitt**y**
pupp**y**

Who are we? We are a famil**y**.

Skill: Recognizing that the letter **y** at the end of a word can make a long **e** sound

page 89

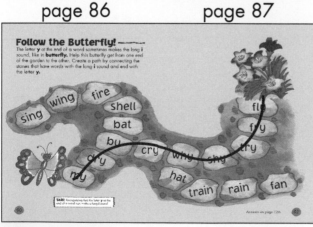

Follow the Butterfly!
The letter **y** at the end of a word sometimes makes the long **i** sound, like in **butterfly**. Help this butterfly get from one end of the garden to the other. Create a path by connecting the stones that have words with the long **i** sound and end with the letter **y**.

sing, wing, fire, shell, fly
bat, fry
by, try
dry, cry, why, shy
my, hat
train, rain, fan

Skill: Recognizing that the letter **y** at the end of a word can make a long **i** sound

page 90

Read All About It!
The letters **-all** make the sound you hear in the word **ball**. Fill in the blanks below with the letters from the box. Use each letter only once. Say the new words you make.

c   f   h   m   t   w

c**all**   m**all**
f**all**   t**all**
h**all**   w**all**

Parents: ...
Skill: Recognizing the **all** sound and spelling pattern

page 91

You Can Write It!
You can make many words with the letters **an**. These words have a short **a** sound and a consonant **n** sound. Look at the pictures and complete each word below with the letters **an**.

m **a n**
v **a n**
h **a n** d
c **a n**
p **a n**
f **a n**

Parents: ...
Skill: Recognizing the **an** sound and spelling pattern

page 92

page 93

That's It!

You can make words with the letters **-at**. These words have a short **a** sound and end with the consonant sound **t**. Look at each picture. Which beginning sound is missing? Use the letters in the box to write the missing beginning sound. You will use each letter once.

b c h m r

b at
h at
m at
r at
c at

page 94

Tell the Name

You can make words with the letters **-ell**, like the word **tell**. The **-ell** pattern uses a short **e** sound and the consonant sound **l**. Look at each picture and find the word in the box that matches. Write the words on the lines.

bell   shell   smell   well   yell

y e l l
w e l l
s m e l l
s h e l l
b e l l

page 95

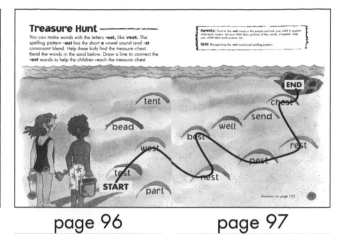

Treasure Hunt

You can make words with the letters **-est**, like **vest**. The spelling pattern **-est** has the short **e** vowel sound and **-st** consonant blend. Help these kids find the treasure chest. Read the words in the sand below. Draw a line to connect the **-est** words to help the children reach the treasure chest.

page 96

page 97

Hidden Words

You can make words with the letters **-ide**, like **slide**. The letters **-ide** have the long **i** sound and the consonant sound **d**. The letter **e** is silent. You don't say it. Write the letters **-ide** to complete each word below. Read the words you've made.

sl i d e
w i d e
t i d e
r i d e
h i d e
s i d e

page 98

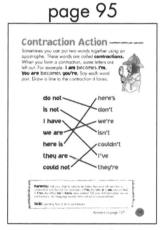

Contraction Action

Sometimes you can put two words together using an apostrophe. These words are called **contractions**. When you form a contraction, some letters are left out. For example, **I am** becomes **I'm**. **You are** becomes **you're**. Say each word pair. Draw a line to the contraction it forms.

do not — here's
is not — don't
I have — we're
we are — isn't
here is — couldn't
they are — I've
could not — they're

page 99

A Web of Words

You can make words with the letters **-ing**, like **string**. The letters **-ing** have the short **i** sound and -ng consonant blend **-ng**. Read the words. Draw a string from the word **string** in the center to words with the **-ing** spelling pattern.

bring   sing   swing
back   **string**   ring
swim   was
king   sign   wing

page 100

Let's Skate!

You can make words with the letters **-ink**, like **rink**. The letters **-ink** have the short **i** sound and the final consonant blend **-nk**. Read each word in the skating rink. Circle the letters **-ink** in each word and say each word.

ink   pink   drink
stink   wink   blink   sink   think

page 101

Between a Rock and a Hard Place

You can make words with the letters **-ock**, like **clock**. The letter **o** makes the short **o** sound. The letters **ck** make the hard **k** sound. Practice writing **-ock** words by following the directions. The pictures will help you.

1. Write the letter **r**: **r** ock
2. Change the r to a **d**: **d** ock
3. Change the d to an **s**: **s** ock
4. Change the s to an **l**: **l** ock
5. Add the letter **c** to the beginning: **c** lock
6. Change the c to a **b**: **b** lock

page 102

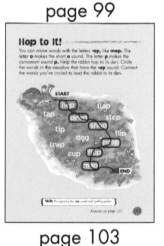

Hop to It!

You can make words with the letters **-op**, like **mop**. The letter **o** makes the short **o** sound. The letter **p** makes the consonant sound **p**. Help the rabbit hop to his den. Circle the words in the meadow that have the **-op** sound. Connect the words you've circled to lead the rabbit to its den.

page 103

Pour It in the Mug!

You can make words with the letters **-ug**, like **bug**. The letter **u** makes the short **u** sound. The letter **g** makes the hard **g** sound. Look at the letters in the mug. Add **-ug** after each letter to make a word.

t ug
h ug
d ug
m ug
j ug
r ug

page 104

What Is It?

You can make words with the letters **-unk**, like **junk**. The letters **nk** make the final consonant blend **nk**. Read each riddle. Answer each riddle with a word from the box.

bunk   junk   sunk   trunk   skunk

1. What the leaky boat did. **s u n k**
2. What is a lot of useless stuff? **j u n k**
3. What animal can make a bad smell? **s k u n k**
4. You put stuff in this. **t r u n k**
5. You might sleep in the top or bottom one. **b u n k**

page 105

A Pirate's Treasure

Most words are made plural by adding the letter **-s** to the end of the word.

1 pirate   2 pirates   1 parrot   2 parrots

Write the letter **-s** on the end of the word if it should be plural.

coin   coin **s**   cow   cow **s**
crown   crown   ring   ring **s**
car   car   hat   hat **s**

page 106

More than One Way

Some words are made plural by adding the letters **-es** to the end of the word.

1 dish   2 dishes   1 lunch   2 lunches

Look at the pictures. Circle the plural form of the word.

(foxes)   fox   bus   (buses)
(glasses)   glass   (bushes)   bush
box   (boxes)   (peaches)   peach

page 107

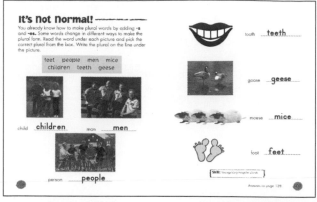

It's not Normal!
You already know how to make plural words by adding -s and -es. Some words change in different ways to make the plural form. Read the word under each picture and pick the correct plural from the box. Write the plural on the line under the picture.

feet people men mice
children teeth geese

tooth — **teeth**
goose — **geese**
mouse — **mice**
foot — **feet**
child — **children**
man — **men**
person — **people**

page 108

Drop the Y!
Words that end in y are made plural by changing the y to an i and adding the letters -es. So one penny becomes five pennies.

1 penny   5 pennies

Look at the pictures and circle the word that matches what you see.

daisy — **daisies**
baby — **babies**
puppy — **puppies**
berry — **berries**

page 109

Look What I Am Doing!
Adding the letters -ing to the end of a word makes the word present tense. The word tells about something that is happening now.

I talk to my teacher.   I am talking to my teacher now.

Look at what each cat is doing. Circle the word in each sentence that has the letters -ing.

page 110

page 111

What the Lion Did
Adding the letters -ed to the end of a word makes the word past tense. Past tense means that a word tells about something that was done before, or in the past.
For example:
Today I talk to my teacher.
Yesterday I talked to my teacher.

Tell what the lion did. Add the letters -ed to each action word.

roar **ed**   jump **ed**   cover **ed**
walk **ed**   splash **ed**

page 112

Who Is the Most?
Adding the letters -est to the end of a word can make the word mean the most. Adding the letters -est helps compare two or more things.
It is cold outside.   It is the coldest day of the year!

Look at the fans at this football game. Label each fan to tell about him or her. Use the words in the box.

loudest saddest tallest youngest

tallest   loudest   youngest   saddest

page 113

Who Is More?
Adding the letters -er to the end of a word can make the word mean more. Adding the letters -er helps people compare two things.
This school is small.   Our school is smaller.

Read about these animals. Circle the word that best compares the animals.

The turtle is (slow, slower) than the cat.
The cat is (softer, soft) than the turtle.
The elephant is (stronger, strong) than the goose.
The goose is (small, smaller) than the elephant.

page 114

Double Up!
Sometimes you need to double the last letter of a word if you add a suffix. For example:

hot hotter hottest

Rewrite these words by doubling the last letter and adding -ed.
stop **stopped**   hop **hopped**

Rewrite these words by doubling the last letter and adding -ing.
run **running**   tug **tugging**

Rewrite these words by doubling the last letter and adding -est.
wet **wettest**   sad **saddest**

page 115

Syllable Sounds
A syllable is the sound contained in a part of a word. Some words only have one syllable. Words like run, go, my, to, bike, and dog have only one syllable. Some words have two syllables. The words have two parts. Window has two parts: win•dow. Giraffe also has two parts: gir•affe. Read the words in the picture. If the word has one syllable, color the section green. If the word has two syllables, color the section orange.

page 116

Splitting Syllables
Words with more than one syllable can be long words. Dividing long words into syllables can help you read these long words. If you see two consonants in the middle of a word, you can often divide the word between those two letters, like rabbit: rab•bit. Read the word for each picture. Draw a line down the middle of the word to show the syllables.

bubble   turkey   pizza
monkey   raccoon   kitten

Bonus:
How many syllables do the words above have? **2**

page 117

Put Them Together
Some words are made up of two words. These words are called compound words. Put the two words together to make a compound word.

foot + ball = **football**
light + house = **lighthouse**
grand + mother = **grandmother**
cow + boy = **cowboy**
gold + fish = **goldfish**

page 118

bath + tub = **bathtub**
skate + board = **skateboard**
air + port = **airport**
bull + frog = **bullfrog**
pop + corn = **popcorn**

page 119

Working with Words
Use everything you have learned about phonics to read the following poem. It's about reading and phonics. Circle the words that rhyme.

Working with words can be lots of fun
Phonics helps me read words by the ton
The world is full of words, so many to know
Words to help me learn and grow
With reading I can learn about lots of stuff
There's so much to read. I can't read enough
I know reading will show me the way
And my reading will grow every day

Hooray! You've completed this book about reading and phonics! Write your name on the line and read the message!

Answers will vary.

IS GREAT AT PHONICS!

page 120

128